Introduction

SEINFELD CROSSWORDS is my second puzzle book dedicated to the hit TV show SEINFELD. I want to thank all the SEINFELD fans who have enjoyed my other book and have written such great reviews. My inspiration has come from them.

This book of crossword puzzles has been a labor of love. There are 50 puzzles which cover 59 episodes. Each puzzle is based on a specific SEINFELD episode and all the clues are for that episode. I even list the season and episode number in the Table of Contents. There are many great websites where you can revisit them if you wish.

I had a blast doing this book and hope it brings many hours of enjoyment.

All my best,

Table Of Contents

The Seinfeld Chronicles S1 E1

Male Unbonding S1 E4

The Jacket S2 E3

The Heart Attack S2 E8

The Baby Shower S2 E10

The Busboy S2 E12

The Note S3 E1

The Library S3 E5

The Tape S3 E8

The Boyfriend/The New Friend S3 E17/18

The Limo S3 E19

The Trip S4 E1/2

The Wallet/The Watch S4 E5/6

The Bubble Boy S4 E7

The Contest S4 E11

The Airport S4 E12

The Pick S4 E13

The Outing S4 E17

The Implant S4 E19/20

The Pilot S4 E23/24

The Mango S5 E1

The Puffy Shirt S5 E2

The Marine Biologist S5 E14

The Stand-In S5 E15

The Raincoats S5 E18/19

The Fire S5 E20

The Hamptons S5 E21

The Opposite S5 E22

The Mom & Pop Store S6 E10

The Race S6 E10

The Highlights of 100 S6 E14/15

The Jimmy S6 E19

The Fusilli Jerry S6 E21

The Understudy S6 E24

The Hot Tub S7 E5

The Soup Nazi S7 E6

The Rye S7 E11

The Cadillac S7 E14/15

The Friars Club S7 E17

The Calzone S7 E20

The Bottle Deposit S7 E21/22

The Invitations S7 E24

The Bizarro Jerry S8 E3

The Abstinence S8 E9

The Yada Yada S8 E19

The Summer of George S8 E22

The Serenity Now S9 E3

The Merv Griffin Show S9 E5

The Strike S9 E10

The Finale S9 E 23/24

Dear Fellow Puzzle Lovers,

Thank you for purchasing this book. I hope it brings you hours of enjoyment.

As a small publishing company, reviews are the lifeblood of our continued success. If you could take a few minutes to leave us a review on Amazon it would be greatly appreciated.

www.oldtownpublishing.com/reviews

Thank you,

Miranda

The Seinfeld Chronicles

Across

3. Original Luncheonette name
6. Stand-up _____
8. It keeps your shirt together
9. Red and green lights, e.g.
11. Not in this episode
13. Jerry's female visitor
14. Set to wed
15. "What men want"

Down

1. JFK for one
2. Jason
4. Trip around the island (2 wds.)
5. Before Kramer
7. Going out with
10. New York Borough
12. Exciting place for clothes

Male Unbonding

Across

3. Jerry's ex-girlfriend
6. "It's not _____, it's me"
7. Cop-out
8. Piggy bank fillers
9. Italian fast food
11. "Laughing all the way to the _____"
12. Call it quits

Down

1. Kramer's new company
2. NY basketball team
4. Lacking tact
5. Dudes
9. Table tennis (2 wds.)
10. Jerry's old "friend"

The Jacket

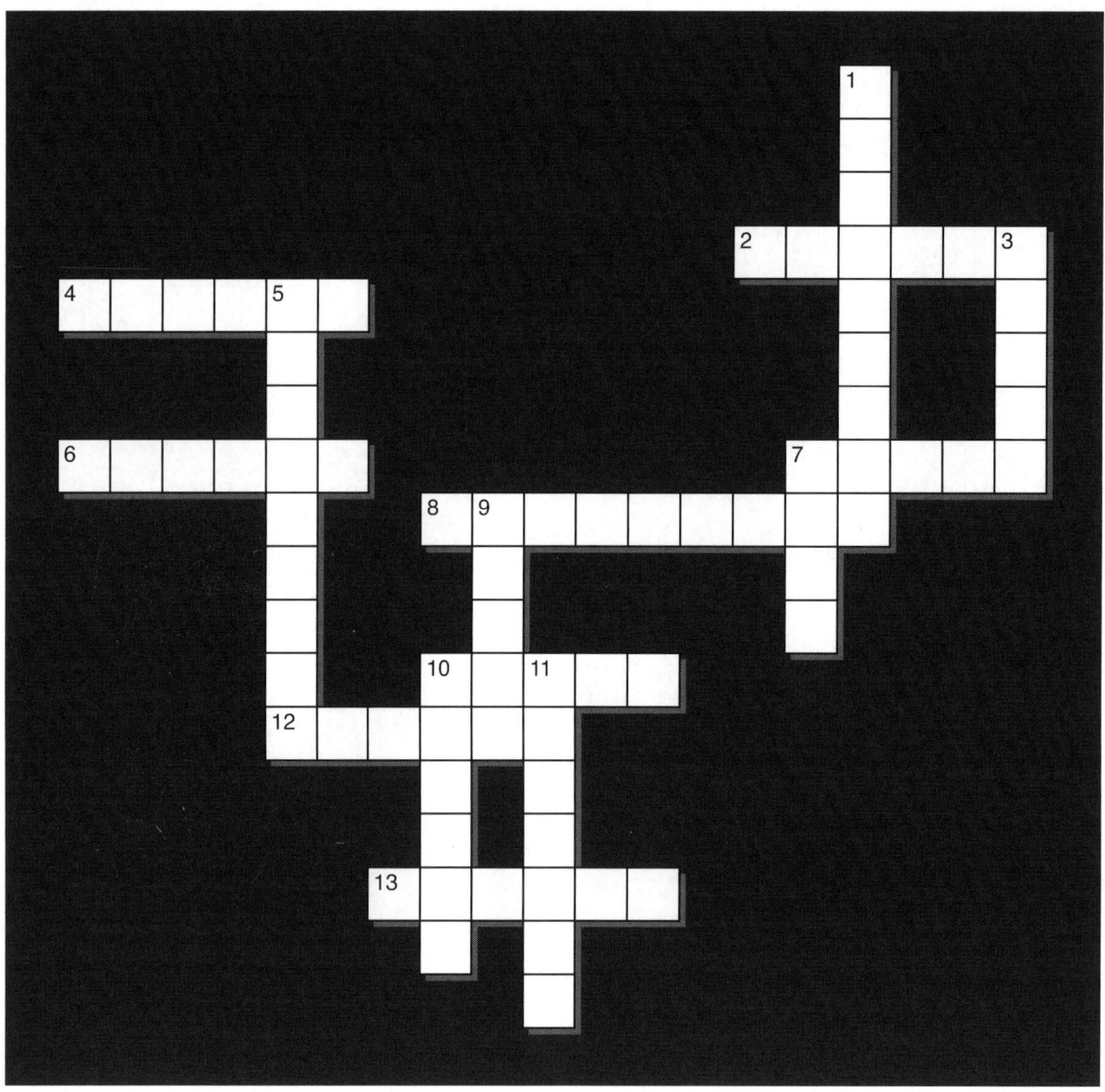

Across

2. _____ on the rocks
4. Part of a suit
6. Dad's profession
7. Soft leather material
8. Pink and white lining (2 wds.)
10. Birds of peace
12. Works for Pendant Publishing
13. Extremely nervous

Down

1. Opening talk
3. "Master of the _____"
5. High-priced
7. Winter weather
9. Elaine's dad
10. Evening repast
11. Ex-soldier

The Heart Attack

Across

2. Can't read a joke he wrote
4. Friend is an herbalist
7. Integrated type of medicine
8. Organ of taste
10. Having a heart attack?
12. Human repair shop
13. "Like flaming _____, Sigmond"
14. Emergency vehicle

Down

1. Frozen dessert (2 wds.)
3. Pharaoh's tomb
5. Dated George's doctor
6. Nonessential throat part
7. Medicine man, e.g.
9. Turned George pink
11. Pleasure peak

The Baby Shower

Across

3. Humiliated by women
5. Payback time
9. Party planner
10. Leslie ruined George's _____ _____ (2 wds.)
12. Real name on the restaurant
13. Rosemary's _____
14. Not broadcast TV

Down

1. Waiting for a delivery
2. John F. _____
4. Kramer to Jerry
6. The "F" in UFO
7. Terrifying dream
8. Gets shot by the FBI
11. Putin's people

The Busboy

Across

2. The perfect bystander
5. Kramer's nickname
8. Green pasta sauce
9. Diner handout
10. Elaine's "friend's" home town
12. Off the payroll
13. Cafe or bistro

Down

1. Residential flat
3. Created a car accident
4. Blaze
5. Purr producer
6. Say you're sorry
7. Table clearer
11. Strong disagreement

The Note

Across

3. Worry that you are gay
6. Health-spa offering
7. Daydream
8. Can't get an appointment
10. He wrote the fake note
11. Said, "I think it moved"

Down

1. The actual name of the coffee shop
2. Dinky _____
4. Evander Holyfield
5. Rubs you the right way
6. Another slang name for homosexual
9. Safeguard for the future
10. Yankee Hall of Famer

The Library

Across

5. Afraid she's getting fired
6. Dates the librarian
7. His old Phys Ed teacher is homeless
9. Overdue fee
10. Workout site
11. "Tropic of _____"
13. Rhyme writing
14. Elaine works at _____ Publishing

Down

1. He's the library policeman
2. Person in charge of books, etc.
3. Prank involving underwear
4. Place where borrowing is encouraged
8. In a book-lover's wallet (2 wds.)
12. "Can't-Stand-Ya"

The Tape

Across

3. Has a crush on Elaine
5. TV show recording medium
9. Comic's repertoire
10. It grows on you
12. Loves his new camera
13. Favorite delivery food

Down

1. Outmoded music recording
2. "Controls the foot" (2 wds.)
4. Beijing is the capital
6. Smutty flicks, e.g.
7. Thin on top
8. X-rated
11. Has a "hot" voice
13. MSNBC alternative

The Boyfriend/The New Friend

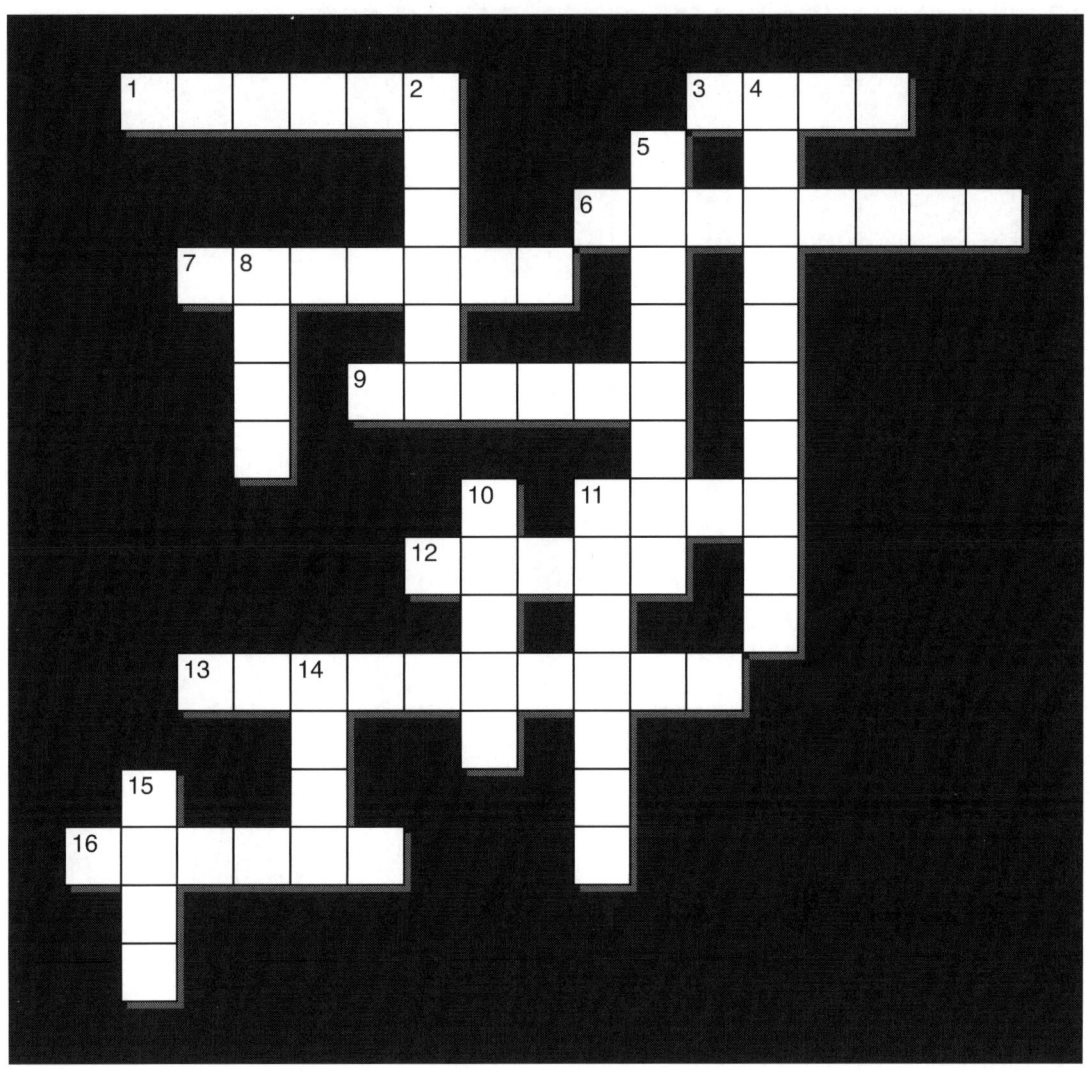

Across

1. "That is one magic _____"
3. Hobbyist
6. The National Pastime
7. Hard habit to kick
9. Wants to be a Latex salesman
11. Newborn child
12. Nervous about his "Man date"
13. LeBron's sport
16. Postal friend

Down

2. Dates a ball player
4. Not working
5. "Seinfeldian" company, _____ industries
8. Relocate furniture
10. _____ Hernandez
11. End a relationship
14. NY Stadium
15. Big Apple baseballers

The Limo

Across

2. The Windy City
3. "Stand-up" kind of guy
6. Thinks Jerry is in the CIA
8. "Dylan Murphy"
9. Dublin's country
12. Public address
13. Raise an objection

Down

1. Hitler supporter
2. Personal driver
4. Head of the Aryan Union
5. Madison Square ____
7. VIP's vehicle
10. Where planes land
11. Upper ____ Side

The Trip

Across

2. Con's confines
4. Kramer's movie (2 wds.)
6. "The Smog ____"
9. Monopoly buy
10. "The ____ Show"
12. Wants to be an actor

Down

1. Famous boulevard
3. 90's hit sitcom
5. 90's Late-night TV host (2 wds.)
6. Air pollution
7. Goes with Jerry to LA
8. Lawbreaker
10. Give waiter gratuity
11. "____ or no-tuck"

The Wallet/The Watch

Across

5. Seinfeld's eccentric relative (2 wds.)
7. Almost blows the deal
8. "SNL" Network
9. Place for bills
10. Where Tampa is
12. First of a TV series
13. _____ Joe Davola
15. Elaine's "boyfriend"

Down

1. Evil hypnotist of fiction
2. Shoelace alternative
3. Haggle or barter
4. Illegal Cubans
6. Jerry's dad
9. Timepiece
11. Wet-weather apparel
14. Takes bone photos

The Bubble Boy

Across

5. Five-alarmer, e.g.
6. Game on a green
8. What credit cards are made of
10. Trivial Pursuit
12. A celebrity might be asked for one
14. Begin to boil

Down

1. Classic chocolate drink brand
2. Pungent bulb
3. Answering machine playback
4. Where to take a stained suit (2 wds.)
7. What a good joke elicits
9. Not Moors
11. Home in the woods
13. George's girl friend

The Contest

Across

2. "John-John" (abbr.) (2 wds.)
4. "Master of my ____"
5. Women's magazine
7. Contest
11. Part of some patients' care (2 wds.)
12. Make a bet
13. Reason for an R rating

Down

1. Workout set to music
3. First one out
5. He was caught … "You know"
6. Chaste
8. Second one out
9. One with no tan lines
10. Mrs. Costanza

The Airport

Across

4. Alternative to JFK Airport
8. Vacation wheels (2 wds.)
10. Trapped in the bathroom
12. Lousy tipper
13. Jewish food custom

Down

1. Aloha state capital
2. Special airport shop (2 wds.)
3. Guest of the state
5. Luggage lugger
6. Stalks an "old friend"
7. Pricey plane section (2 wds.)
9. Runway worker
11. "____ Magazine"

The Pick

Across

3. Underwear model
5. Schnoz
7. Alternative to Armani
9. "I am not an _____"
11. Exposed more then she wanted to
13. December holiday

Down

1. Subject of Vogue Magazine
2. Goes to a therapist
4. Kramer's perfume idea (2 wds.)
5. Infant bottle topper
6. She dumped George
8. Called a picker
10. Has a crush on Elaine
12. Holiday greeting to many

The Outing

Across

2. George's "porno actor" name (2 wds.)
6. Formal meeting with questions
8. Fear of being gay
10. Two-Line _____
12. The "G" part of LGBTQ
14. His parents freaked out
15. Exposed

Down

1. Manhattan school
3. George's current GF
4. Shower alternative
5. Annual celebration
7. "Not that there's anything _____ with it"
9. Place for some skeletons
11. Listen secretly
13. Newsperson

The Implant

Across

3. Sweatbox
5. A "double-dipper"
7. "They're _____ ... and they're spectacular!"
8. Jerry's current GF
10. Fitness center (2 wds.)
13. Counterfeit
14. Novelist

Down

1. Burial ceremony
2. Respond to the alarm
4. Embed surgically
6. Accidentally touched them
9. Workout consequence
11. Dracula's bed
12. Chicken choices

The Pilot

Across

1. Full-bosomed
6. "All backed up"
8. Close female relatives
11. NBC prez is obsessed with her
13. Cockpit boss
15. Group that protects the environment
16. Man of many parts

Down

2. Robbed
3. She takes orders
4. Manservant
5. Pre-exercise exercise (2 wds.)
7. Dried grapes
9. Give the go-ahead (2 wds.)
10. Hypochondriac
12. "_____ Semper Tyrannis"
14. New show's name

The Mango

Across

5. Feeling dysfunctional
6. Usual meeting place
8. Creamy Italian dish
9. A particular action or deed
11. Not genuine
12. Meryl Streep is a great one

Down

1. Aphrodisiac
2. Kind of tension
3. Doesn't satisfy Elaine
4. Relation between mates
7. Banned by a fruit store
9. Fuzzy fruit
10. Exciting conclusion

The Puffy Shirt

Across

4. Speaks softly (2 wds.)
6. React to a joke
8. Fund-raising event
10. _____ Stiller
12. Long John Silver, for one
14. They made you

Down

1. Morning TV show
2. Change location
3. Showing something off
5. Swollen
7. Ridiculous
9. Living back with parents
11. They travel around the clock
13. Wrinkle remover

The Marine Biologist

Across

3. "A ____ in one, huh?"
6. Elaine's boss
8. Man of the hour
11. Moscow native
12. Titleist, e.g. (2 wds.)
13. Wheels for big wheels
14. Sandy shore

Down

1. Ocean giant
2. Annoying sound
4. "War and _____"
5. Reunion crowd
7. "Golden Boy"
9. Electronic info holder
10. Says he is a marine biologist

The Stand-In

Across

5. Alternative to talking
7. Kramer's little friend
9. Like an elephant or rhino
11. Public transport
12. Star's sub (2 wds.)

Down

1. Cheers up a friend
2. "He _____ it out"
3. Sometimes we need a good one
4. Heighteners
6. Can't make a commitment
8. Brought it to light
10. Not Costello
11. Uninteresting

The Raincoats

Across

3. Young boy's role model (2wds.)
4. Sunshine State city
5. George's dad
8. Close talker
9. Good-natured
10. Shirts and shorts
11. Like fine wine
13. Sweater eating insects
14. French money

Down

1. Spanish seafood and rice dish
2. Vacation on a vessel
4. No-no during Schindler's List (2wds.)
6. Seattle garb
7. The City of Light
9. Is a tattletale
12. Parisian Architect

The Fire

Across

2. Where comics work
4. Photog's request
5. Comic's nightmare
9. Baby toe
10. Infused with enthusiasm
12. Critic's write-up

Down

1. Torment a comic
2. Entertainer at a kid's party
3. Knucklehead
6. Make reservations
7. Juvenile
8. Street thief
9. Going to publish Kramer's book
11. Where there's smoke

The Hamptons

Across

2. Where to play marco polo
6. He's a Poacher
7. Part of a BLT
8. Seafood delicacy
9. Washing woe
10. Unattractive
12. Weekend getaway for New Yorkers
14. What "TGIF" anticipates

Down

1. On the up and up
3. Restaurant freebee
4. Without a shirt
5. Member of the AMA
9. Beachgoer's souvenir
11. Scrambles some "non-kosher" eggs
13. Sun blocker

The Opposite

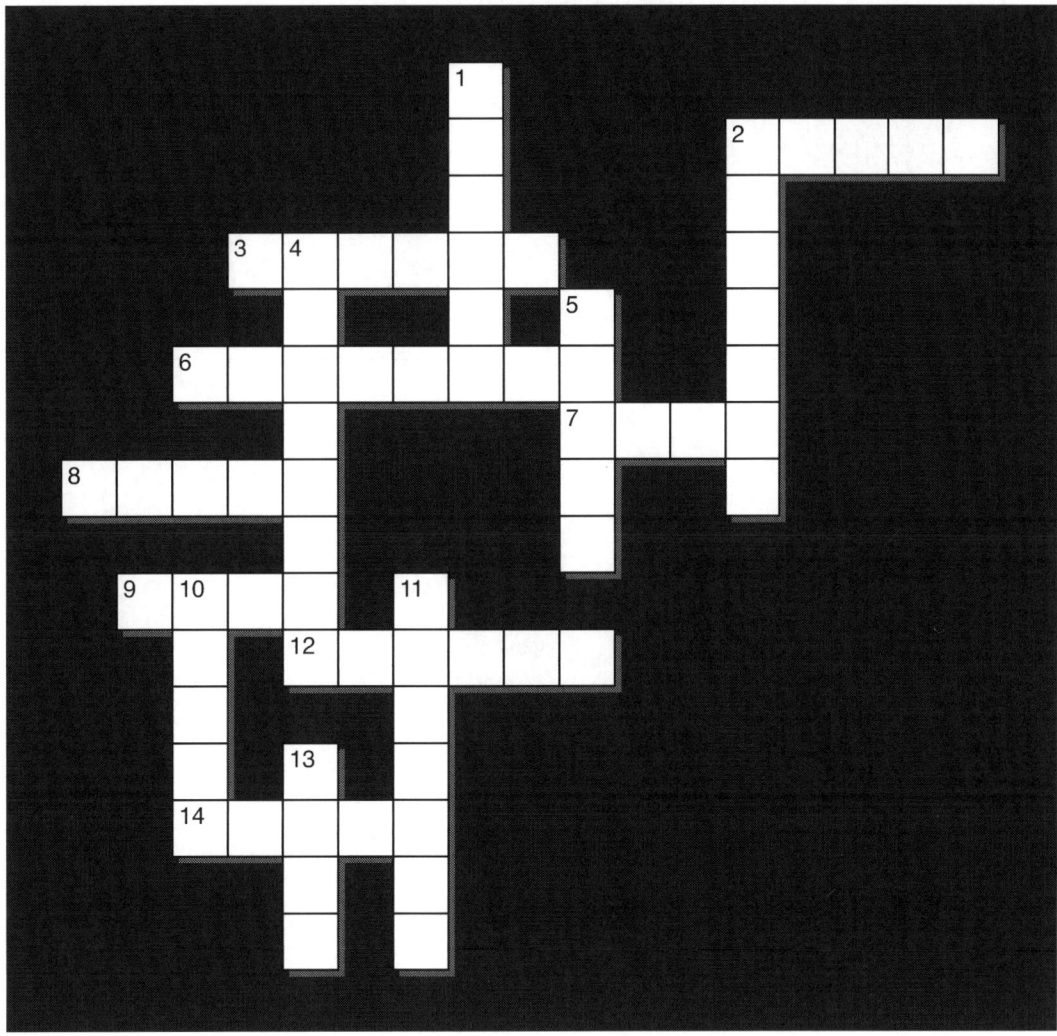

Across

2. Date night option
3. Kramer's _____ Table Book
6. They have a "yen" for business
7. Uncouth
8. First name in TV talk
9. Saliva
12. Jujyfruits get her in trouble
14. Worker's reward

Down

1. Cold symptom
2. Speaks unclearly
4. Contrary
5. "Even-Steven" is his new nickname
10. It ends with a show of hands
11. George's new job
13. Elaine's old roommate

The Mom & Pop Store

Across

2. Thanksgiving Day Parade sponsor
3. Jazz from New Orleans
5. Texas club paid Jerry in these
6. One who knows the drill
8. Cobbler's creation
10. Convinced to buy a LeBaron
11. Festive occasion

Down

1. Like some seats in a stadium
2. Elaine's boss (2 wds.)
4. Famous Woodpecker
7. Gym wear
9. "Midnight Cowboy"
10. Kind of sale

The Race

Across

4. Bay of Pigs figure
6. Plays Santa
7. Where the best cigars come from
9. How Jerry wins
11. Mandarin or Cantonese
13. Santa's helper
14. A Putin pal

Down

1. Jerry's favorite comic book
2. Clark Kent's co-worker
3. Track event
5. George's favorite fake profession
8. Fastest kid in school
9. "I _____ not to run"
10. Present time?
12. Blacklisted from delivery

The Highlights of 100

Across

2. Candy in a dispenser
4. Kramer wants people to make their own
7. Obnoxious comedian friend
9. Like old tires
11. "Does it" with the cleaning lady
12. Drops one into a surgery (2wds.)
15. Spicy sauce
16. What the new show is about

Down

1. George double-dipped it
2. Mall adjacent (2 wds.)
3. The "P" of USPS
5. Swirly Jewish cake
6. "The _____ ate your baby"
8. "It's not _____, it's me"
9. Pakistani restaurant owner
10. Name rhymes with a female body part
13. "Spending the _____ is optional"
14. Gives Jerry his Astronaut pen

The Jimmy

Across

4. Type of gas used by dentist
6. Takes others' stuff
8. Showy basket
9. Appears mentally challenged
10. Sexy mag
13. Run at the mouth
14. Ceremonious event

Down

1. Able Mentally Challenged Adults, for short
2. "The Velvet Fog" (2 wds.)
3. Kung Pao _____
5. "The Tonight Show" host Fallon
7. Vertical leap
11. Song, "When You're _____"
12. Perspire

The Fusilli Jerry

Across

2. Had an eye job
3. Elaine's BF
4. Loves "The Move"
7. Cheat sheets (2 wds.)
9. Fender-bender-mender
11. Part of "The Move"
12. Having sex problems

Down

1. Has a special "Move"
3. Personalized license _____
5. Proctologist
6. Corkscrew-shaped pasta
8. Seeing other people
10. Kramer's first name

The Understudy

Across

2. Coney Island, Pebble, etc
4. Red Cross, e.g.
6. Romantic fling
9. "Rochelle, _____"
11. Seoul soul
12. "Black & White"
13. "The Divine Miss M"

Down

1. "Underhanded" sport
3. Listen in
4. One who weeps
5. Jerry's team
7. Bring comfort to
8. Croon
10. Meets her future boss

The Hot Tub

Across

4. Gets writer's block
6. Elaine's boss
8. Long run
10. Blew a fuse
14. Texas baseball team
15. Good-natured swear

Down

1. Not on time
2. George's boss
3. Overly cautious
5. Warning device
7. Traveler's stop
9. Place to relax (2 wds.)
11. Track athlete
12. Good, long bath
13. Himalayan Walking _____

The Soup Nazi

Across

2. Treat with contempt
3. "Schindler's List" villain
5. He's mugged
7. Director Reiner
8. Made-up endearment
9. Guidelines
11. Chooses soup over a woman
13. Soup container

Down

1. Pisses off the chef
4. A large wardrobe
6. Chef's creation
7. Eye for an eye
10. "Goo Goo Gaa Gaa," e.g. (2 wds.)
12. "No soup for _____"

The Rye

Across

2. Should be served after dinner
4. George's future in-laws
8. Stinky horse sounds
9. Dating a musician
10. Word of mouth
14. Hansom cab driver
15. Non-Jewish

Down

1. Sculpture material
3. "____ -A-Reeno"
4. Kind of bread
5. Woodwind instrument
6. Take without asking
7. Bebop, e.g.
11. Schnitzer's
12. Spouse to be
13. "____ and Heavy"

The Cadillac

Across

2. Legal tender
6. Owned apartment
8. Kind of TV
9. Suspect defense
11. Film award
12. Untruth
13. Fling
14. It takes a bow
15. Getting "gold digger" instincts

Down

1. Accuse of misconduct
3. Senior dinner special (2 wds.)
4. Jerry's parents home state
5. Betrothed
7. Cheater
10. "My Cousin Vinnie" actress

The Friars Club

Across

3. Not hearing
7. Thrown in the river
8. Potter's field
10. Hit the hay
12. Sets up double date
13. Mona Lisa painter

Down

1. New York City river
2. Blazer, e.g.
4. Shopper's guide
5. Elite club for entertainers
6. Tries the hearing aid
9. Pat Cooper
11. Merger of a sort
12. Capone, e.g.

The Calzone

Across

1. Gratuity
6. Goes on a "non-date"
8. Burnt his clothes
9. Small change
12. Order from Domino's
13. Jerry's girlfriend is one
14. Yankee ____

Down

2. Calzones origin
3. Bad ones come from Peru
4. Doesn't work in the rain
5. Steinbrenner's lunch buddy
7. Washer's partner
10. Ethnic of Costanza
11. Kind of ticket

The Bottle Deposit

Across

3. Sale by bids
7. Petula Clark hit
8. On a big project
9. High-speed scene
10. Caddies carry them
12. Oil change place (2wds.)
13. Highway hauler

Down

1. Grease monkey
2. May celebration (2 wds.)
4. Work the land
5. Genie's home
6. Game on a green
11. President #35, for short
12. His car gets stolen

The Invitations

Across

2. Agreement
4. Become extinct
7. Hates Jerry's GF
8. "ER" setting
9. Sticky substance
10. Between lunch and dinner
11. Confrontation
13. Wedding contract, for short

Down

1. Susan's his Fiancé
2. Toxic thing
3. Met someone just like him
5. George starts doing it
6. "First _____ Club"
8. Word of welcome
12. Stingy

The Bizarro Jerry

Across

1. "The Forbidden _____"
4. A place to "go"
9. Hit sitcom
11. Chooses the other world
12. "_____ hands"
13. Catwalk walkers
14. Opposite of Superman

Down

2. Taking care of business, for short
3. Well behaved
5. Other diner
6. "Tastes like an old sponge"
7. Curator's place
8. Has a "job"
10. Stomach woe

The Abstinence

Across

6. Getting dumber
7. Can't do it indoors
8. Young Yankee in this episode
10. Jackie Chiles's profession
11. Katy to Jerry
12. Poke full of holes
13. Professional pursuit

Down

1. Old friend of Elaine's (2 wds.)
2. Picture in Times Square
3. Women must have it
4. No sex for 6 weeks
5. The "kissing disease"
8. Alex Trebek's domain
9. Not a full doctor yet
11. School gathering

The Yada Yada

Across

3. Narrow-minded sort
6. Take for one's own
7. Lobster soup
8. Offends Tim
9. Church title
10. Tim Whatley is one
11. Guest star, _____ Messing

Down

1. Transgress
2. Outing for four (2 wds.)
4. She yada yada-ed sex
5. Calls Jerry an "anti-dentite"
8. Whatley became _____ for the jokes
10. Friend of Snow White

The Summer of George

Across

4. Given the boot
5. Ask to a party
7. Recovery center
10. Jerry's dating helper
11. Full of snark
13. "There's no business like _____ business"

Down

1. Gets in a "cat fight"
2. Famous theater eatery
3. Raquel _____
4. Flying toy disk
6. Cuckoo
8. Sleeve fillers
9. Office copy
12. Kramer "won" one

The Serenity Now

Across

3. "Hoochie ____ "
7. Feeling emotional
9. Peace of mind
10. Parents' borough
11. ____ mitzvah
13. Kissed by 13 year old

Down

1. Frank's new biz
2. Bares his feelings
4. Fit to be tied
5. Cassette
6. Non-Jewish woman
7. Lippman religion
8. Stadium sound
11. Cheap gift
12. Synagogue leader

The Merv Griffin Show

Across

2. Drugs his GF
5. Nut hoarder
6. Animal MD
9. Plays with the Easy Bake Oven
10. Sweeps week concern
12. "Black _____ Down"
13. Vintage playthings

Down

1. Shows home movies
3. Acts as TV host
4. Breath mint brand (2 wds.)
5. One who moves silently behind people
7. Late-nite TV fare (2 wds.)
8. Urban flock
11. Toy soldier (2 wds.)

The Strike

Across

3. George's boss
5. Union action
8. Bowling feat
10. Fake number to denim vest guy
12. "A _____ for the rest of us"
13. Lox partner

Down

1. Forces George to fight
2. Aluminum _____
4. Creates the fake "Human Fund"
6. "Dr. Van Nostrand"
7. Batman villain (2 wds.)
8. "Feats of _____"
9. Eight-day Jewish holiday
11. Gang brawl

The Finale

Across

4. Louvre locale
5. _____ Samaritan Law
6. " _____ face-off"
8. It's going to be "on-the-air"
9. Water in his ear
12. TV reporter
13. TV Network
14. Lockup

Down

1. Courtroom event
2. Spectator
3. Tell all
5. Jury verdict
7. Shawshank
8. Private kind of airplane
10. Vacation spot
11. "The King Of _____ "

SOLUTIONS

The Seinfeld Chronicles

Across:
3. PETES
6. COMEDY
8. BUTTON
9. SIGNALS
11. ELAINE
13. LAURA
14. ENGAGED
15. WOMEN

Down:
1. AIR
2. ALSO
3. POOR
4. BASTARD
5. KESSLER
7. DATING
8. BAD
10. MANHATTAN
11. ERADE
12. LAUNDRY

Male Unbonding

Across:
3. ELAINE
6. YOU
7. EXCUSE
8. PENNIES
9. PIZZA
11. BANK
12. BREAKUP

Down:
1. KRAMER
2. KIMBRK (?)
4. RUDY
5. MEN
9. PINGPONG
10. JOEL
11. BALL

The Jacket

Across:
- 2. SCOTCH
- 4. JACKET
- 6. WRITER
- 7. SUEDE
- 8. CANDYCANE
- 10. DOVES
- 12. ELAINE
- 13. GEORGE

Down:
- 1. MONOLOGUE
- 3. HOUSE
- 5. EXPENSIVE
- 7. SNOW
- 9. ALTNNER (ALTERNATE)
- 11. VETERAN

The Heart Attack

Across:
- 2. JERRY
- 4. KRAMER
- 7. HOLISTIC
- 8. TONGUE
- 10. GEORGE
- 12. HOSPITAL
- 13. GLOBES
- 14. AMBULANCE

Down:
- 1. ICECREAM
- 3. PYRAMID
- 5. ELAINE
- 6. TONSIL
- 9. TEA
- 11. ORGASM
- 12. HEALER

The Baby Shower

Across
3. GEORGE
5. REVENGE
9. ELAINE
10. REDSHIRT
12. OMS
13. BABY
14. CABLE

Down
1. PREGNANT
2. KENNEDY
4. NIGGA (NIG...)
6. FLYING
7. NIGHTMARE
8. JERRY
11. RUSSIANS
13. BMARE

The Busboy

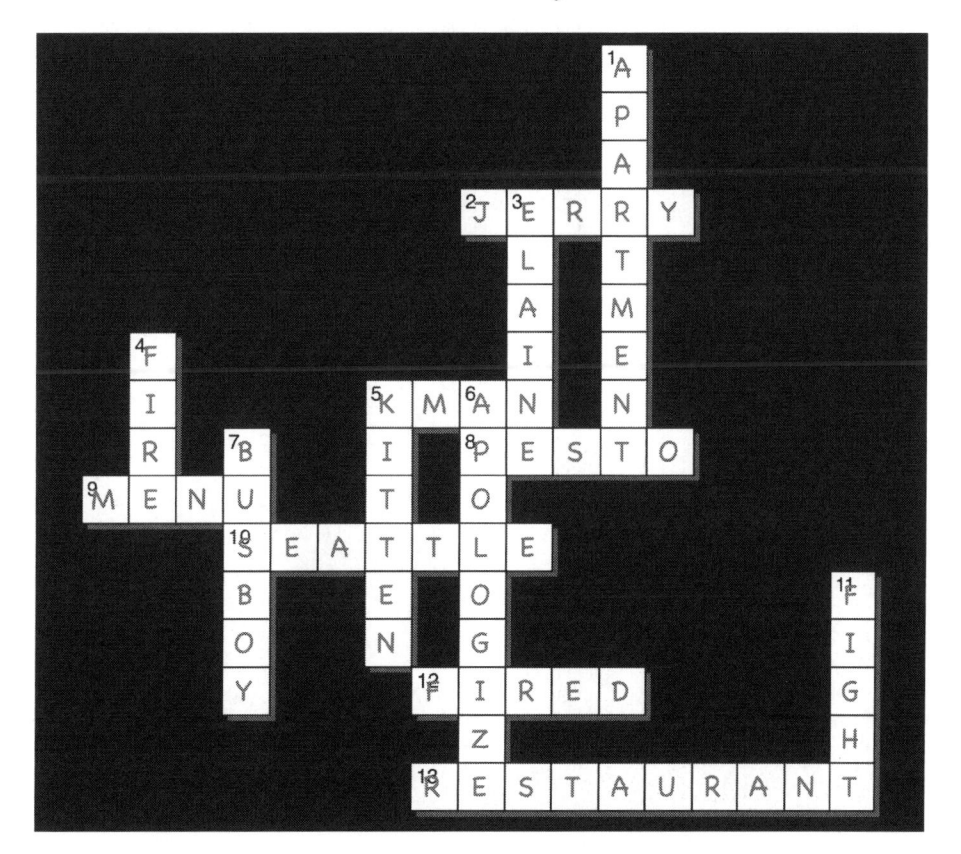

Across
2. JERRY
8. PESTO
9. MENU
10. SEATTLE
12. FIRED
13. RESTAURANT

Down
1. APARTMENT
3. ELAINE
4. FIR
5. KITTEN
6. ANOOG
7. BUSBOY
8. POOG
11. FIGH

The Note

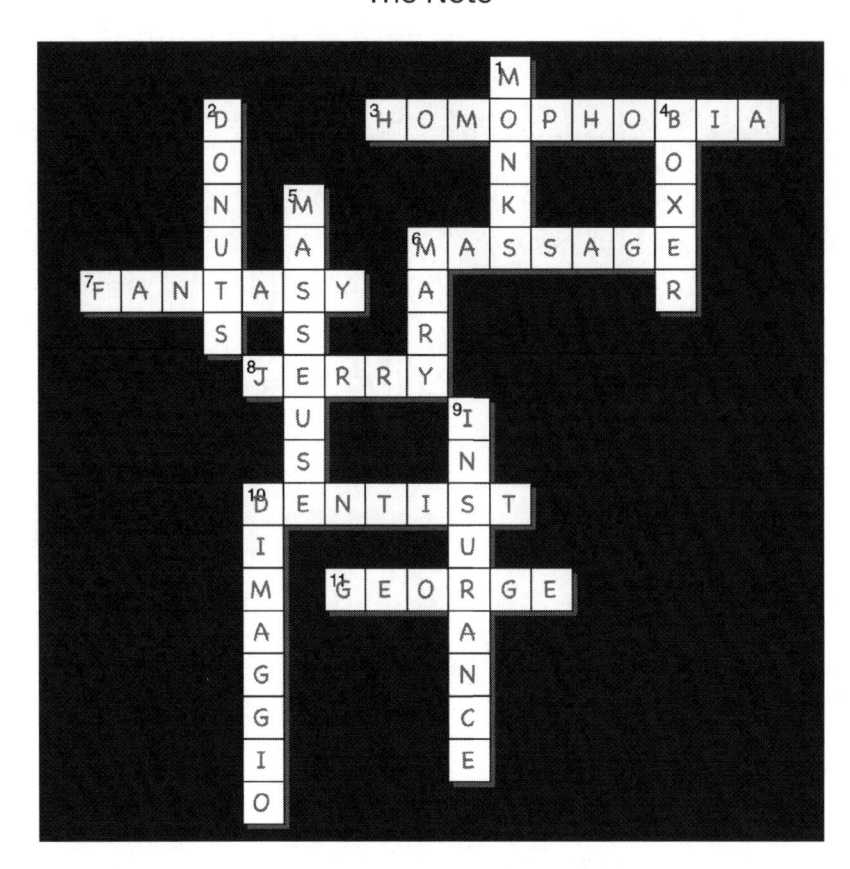

							¹M				
	²D				³H	O	M	O	P	H	O	⁴B	I	A
	O						O					O
	N			⁵M			N					X
	U			A		⁶M	A	S	S	A	G	E	R
⁷F	A	N	T	A	S	Y						R
	S			S		A					
			⁸J	E	R	R	Y			
			U					⁹I	
		¹⁰D	E	N	T	I	S	T	
		I						N	
		M			¹¹G	E	O	R	G	E
		A						A	
		G						N	
		G						C	
		I						E	
		O							

The Library

Across:
5. ELAINE
6. KRAMER
7. GEORGE
9. FINE
10. GYM
11. CANCER
13. POETRY
14. PENDANT

Down:
1. BOOKMAN
2. LIBRARIAN
3. WED
4. LIBRARY
8. LIBRABA (LIBRARY-related)
12. COSTANZA

The Tape

									¹C
									A
							²B		S
							I		S
						³G	E	O	R	G	E
				⁴C		T			T
				H		O			T
			⁵V	I	D	E	O	T	A	⁶P
	⁷B		⁸S	N						O
⁹M	A	T	E	R	I	A	L		¹⁰H	A	I	R
	L		X							N
	D		Y							O
	¹¹E	L								
	¹²K	R	A	M	E	R				
	I		E							
	¹³C	H	I	N	E	S	E			
	N		E							
	N									

The Boyfriend / The New Friend

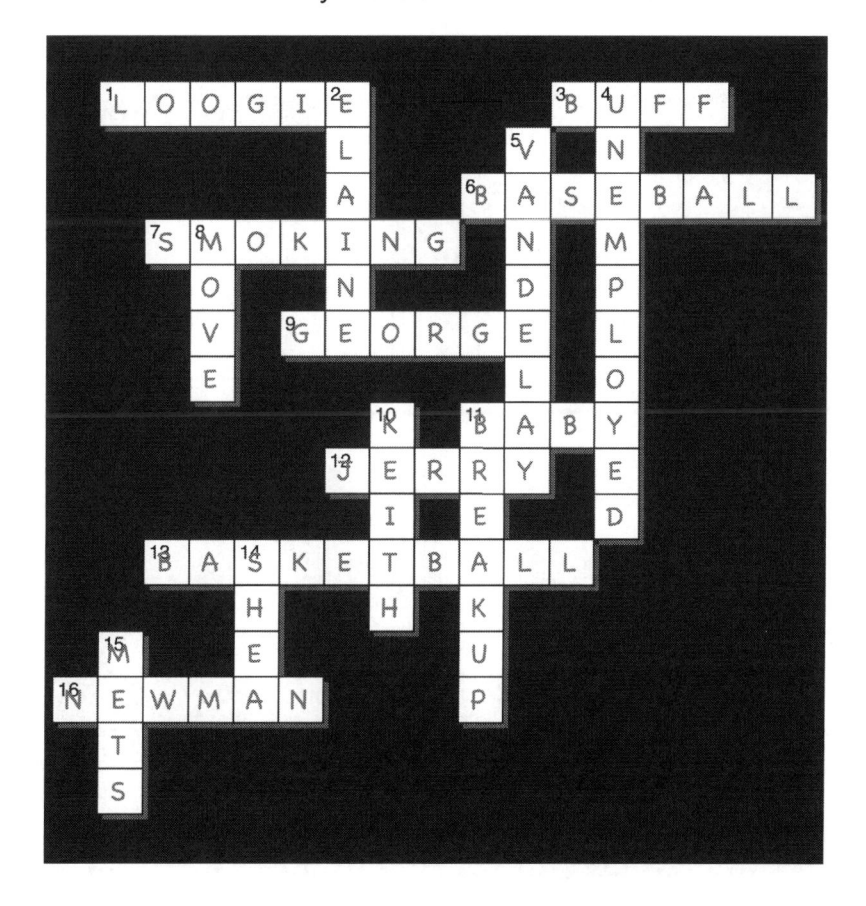

¹L	O	O	G	I	²E			³B	⁴U	F	F
					L		⁵V		N		
					A		⁶B	A	S	E	B	A	L	L
⁷S	⁸M	O	K	I	N	G		N		M	
	O				N			D		P	
	V			⁹G	E	O	R	G	E	L	
	E							L		O	
			¹⁰R		¹¹B	A	B	Y	
			¹²J	E	R	R	Y		E	
			I		E				D	
	¹³B	A	¹⁴S	K	E	T	B	A	L	L
			H		H			K		
	¹⁵M		E					U		
¹⁶N	E	W	M	A	N			P		
	T									
	S									

The Limo

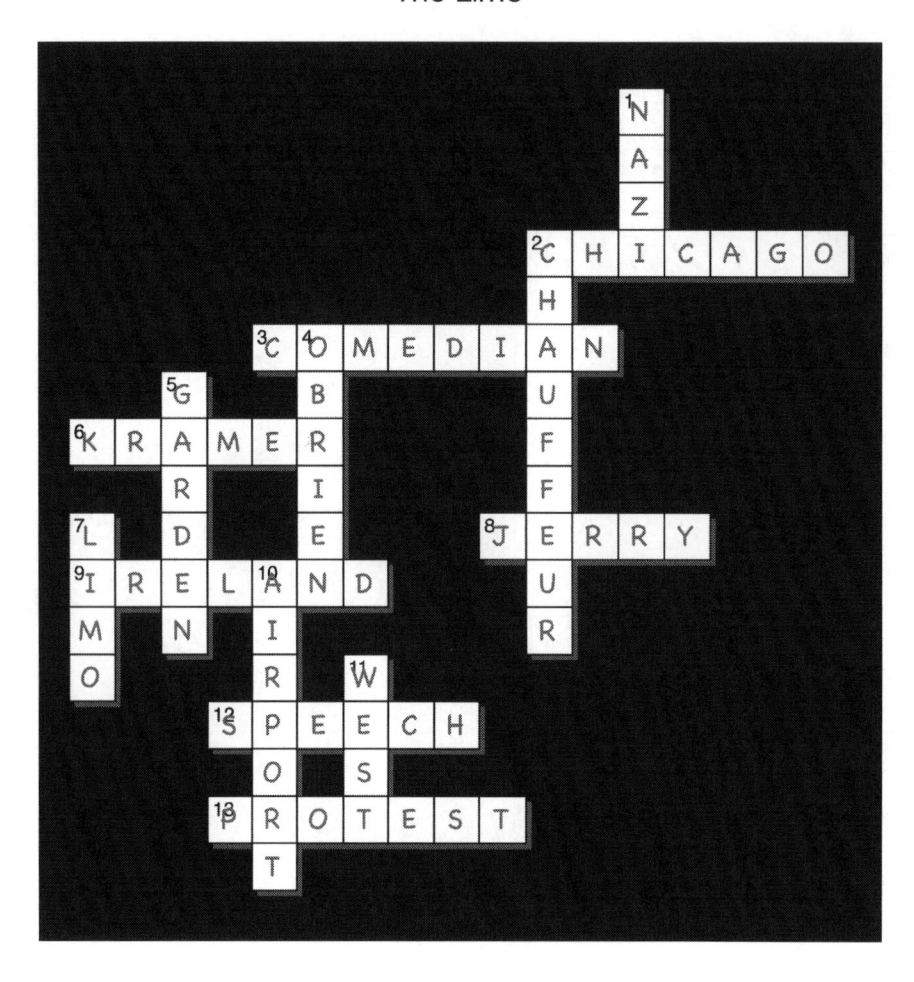

The Trip

The Wallet / The Watch

Across:
- 5. UNCLELEO
- 7. GEORGE
- 8. NBC
- 9. WALLET
- 10. FLORIDA
- 12. PILOT
- 13. CRAZY
- 15. KRAMER

Down:
- 1. SEVEN
- 2. VELCRO
- 3. NEGOTIATE
- 4. CIGARS
- 6. MARRY
- 9. WAITAT
- 11. RAINCOAT
- 14. XRAY

The Bubble Boy

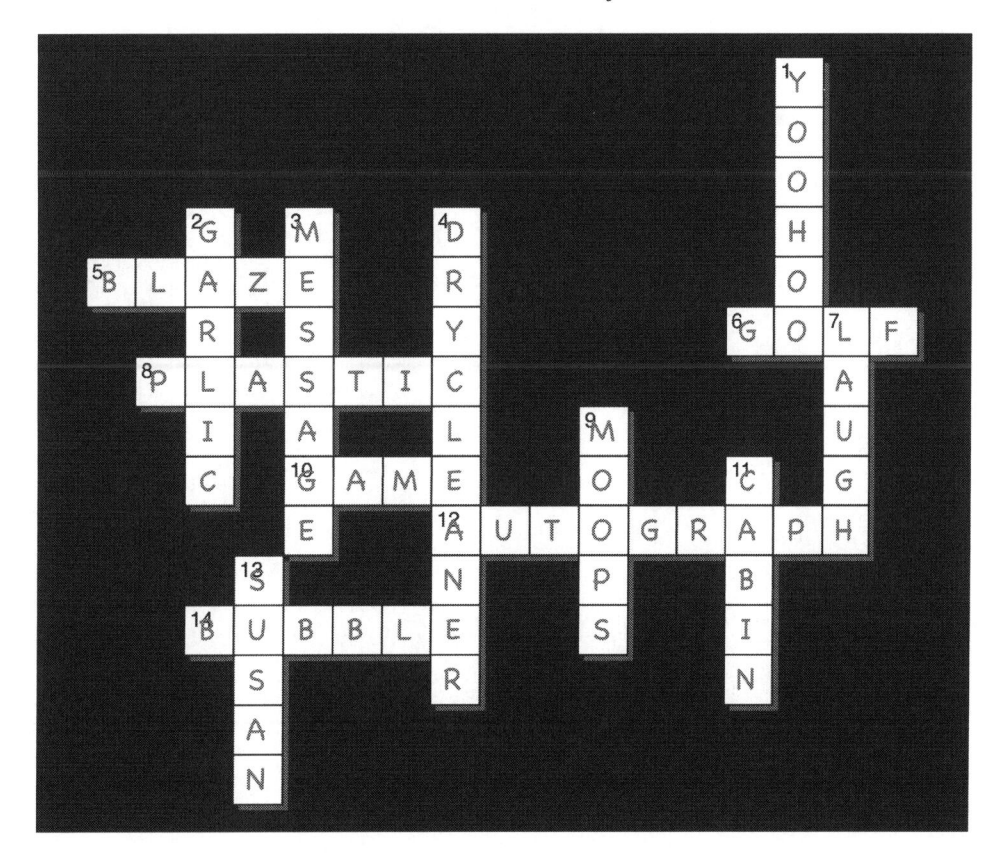

Across:
- 5. BLAZE
- 6. GOLF
- 8. PLASTIC
- 10. GAME
- 12. AUTOGRAPH
- 14. BUBBLE

Down:
- 1. YOOHOO
- 2. GBARS (GEARS?)
- 3. MESSALE
- 4. DRY
- 7. LAUGH
- 9. MOPPS
- 11. CABIN
- 13. SUSAN

The Contest

								¹A
								E
	²J	F	³K		J			R
			R		O			O
			A		B			B
		⁴D	O	M	A	I	N	I
			E					C
	⁵G	L	A	M	O	U	R	S
	E					⁶V		
	⁷C	O	M	P	⁸E	T	I	T	I	O	N	⁹N
¹⁰E					R			I		U
¹¹S	P	O	N	G	E	B	A	T	H		D
T					E		L				I
E							I				S
¹²W	A	G	E	R			N				T
L							E	
L								
¹³S	E	X						

The Airport

¹H
O
N
O
²D	³P
⁴L	A	G	U	A	R	D	I	A
U		T		I					⁵S
L		Y		S		⁶K		K		⁷F
U		F		O		R		Y		I
		⁸R	E	N	T	A	L	C	A	R
		E		E		M		A		S			⁹M
		¹⁰G	E	O	R	G	E	R		T			O
						E		P		C	¹¹T		D
						R			¹²E	L	A	I	N	E
									A		M		L
								¹³K	O	S	H	E	R
									S

The Pick

The Outing

The Implant

The Pilot

The Mango

The Puffy Shirt

The Marine Biologist

The Stand-In

The Raincoats

Across:
3. BIGBROTHER
4. MIAMI
5. F
8. AARON
9. NICE
10. CLOTHES
11. VINTAGE
13. MOTHS
14. FRANCS

Down:
1. PAELLA
2. CRUISE
6. RAINCOAT
7. PARIS
12. EIFFEL
13. MA

(Completed crossword grid with the following filled letters:)

- 3 Across: BIGBROTHER
- 4 Across: MIAMI
- 5 Across: F
- 6 Across: RANK
- 8 Across: AARON
- 9 Across: NICE
- 10 Across: CLOTHES
- 11 Across: VINTAGE
- 13 Across: MOTHS
- 14 Across: FRANCS

The Fire

- 1 Down: HECK
- 2 Across: CLUB
- 3 Down: BOZ
- 4 Across: SMILE
- 5 Across: BOM
- 6 Down: BOO
- 7 Down: K
- 8 Down: MIGGR
- 9 Across: PINKY
- 10 Across: PUMPED
- 11 Down: FIRE
- 12 Across: REVIEW
- Down: PENDANT
- Down: CLOWN

The Hamptons

The Opposite

The Mom & Pop Store

The Race

The Highlights of 100

The Jimmy

The Fusilli Jerry

```
            ¹J
      ²E S T E L L E
            R
            R
      ³P U D D Y
      L
      A
      T
      ⁴E L ⁵A I N E         ⁶F
⁷C R I B N O T E S          U
            S               S
            S       ⁸D      S
            ⁹M E ¹⁰C H A N I C
            A    O
            N    T
                 ¹¹S W I R L
                 M       I
            ¹²G E O R G E
```

The Understudy

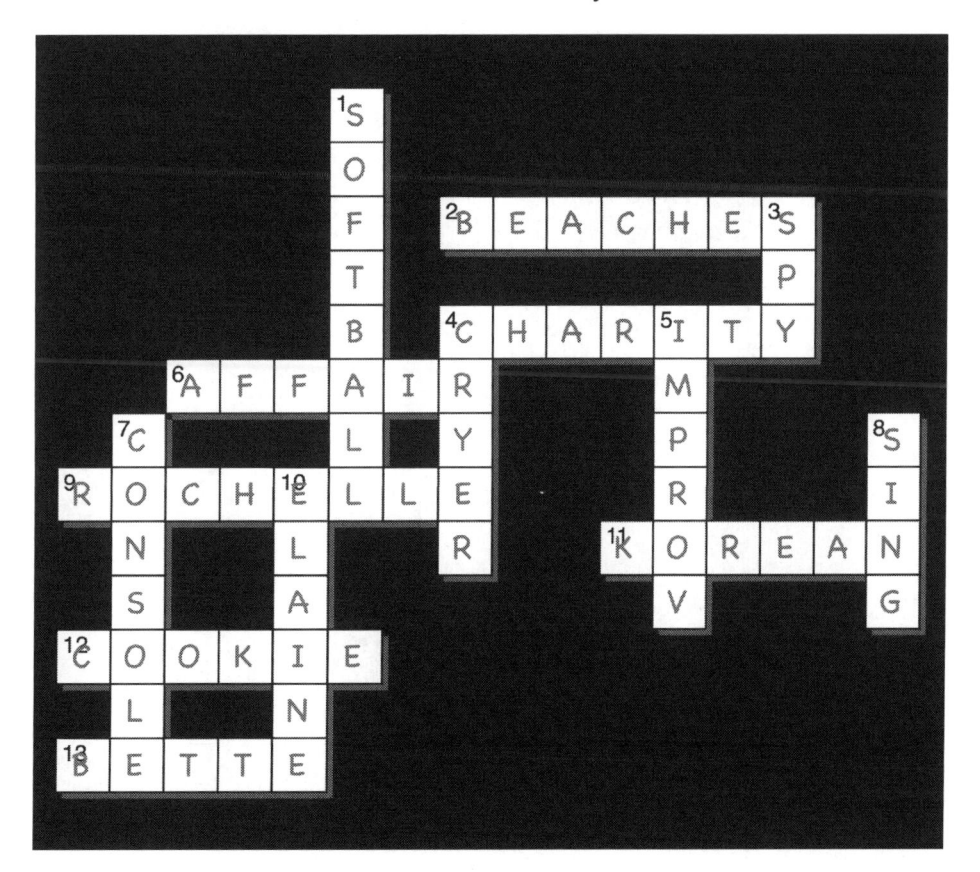

```
              ¹S
              O
              F
              T         ²B E A C H E ³S
              B                     P
              ⁴C H A R ⁵I T Y
      ⁶A F F A I R      M
         ⁷C      L  Y   P       ⁸S
      ⁹R O C H ¹⁰E L L E R       I
         N      L       ¹¹K O R E A N
         S      A       V         G
         ¹²C O O K I E
         L      N
         ¹³B E T T E
```

The Hot Tub

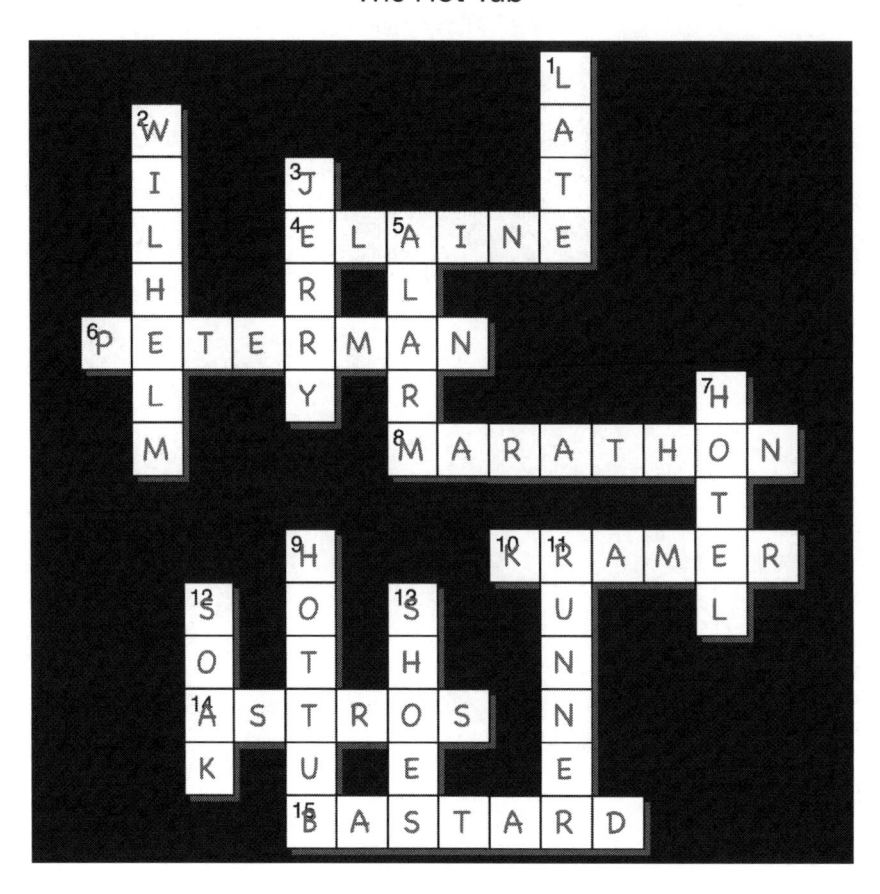

						¹L
	²W		³J			A
	I		⁴E	⁵A	I	N	E
	L		R	L		E
	H		R	L		
⁶P	E	T	E	R	M	A	N
	L		Y	R			⁷H
	M			⁸M	A	R	A	T	H	O	N
			⁹H		¹⁰K	¹¹R	A	M	E	R
	¹²S		O		¹³S	U			T
	O		T		H	N			E
¹⁴A	S	T	R	O	S	N			L
	K		U		E	E
		¹⁵B	A	S	T	A	R	D

The Soup Nazi

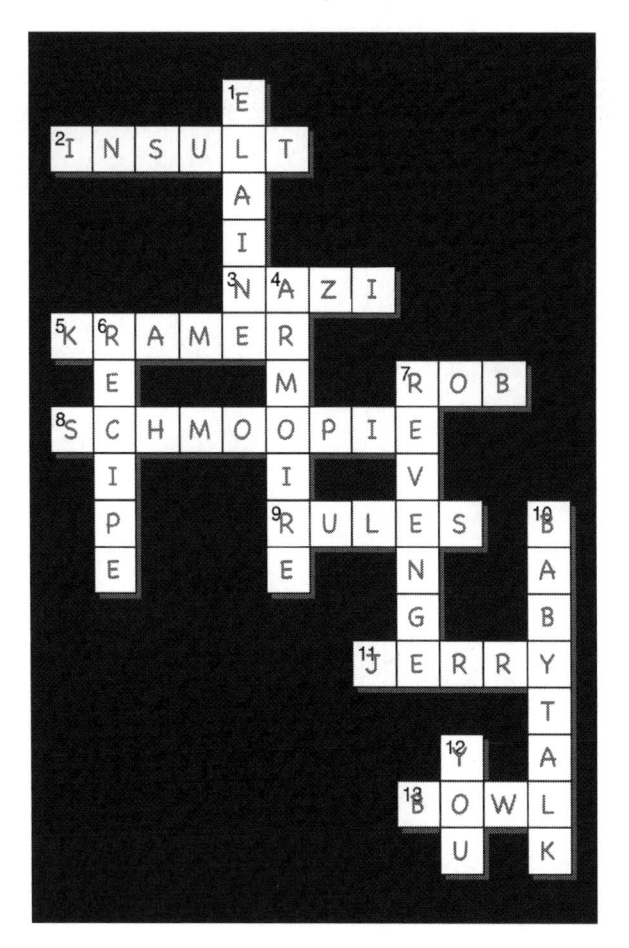

¹E — INSULT — NAI — ³N ⁴AZI — ⁵K⁶RAMER — E M ⁷ROB — ⁸SCHMOOPIE — I I V — P ⁹RULES ¹⁰B — E E N A — G B — ¹¹JERRY — T — ¹²Y A — ¹³BOWL — U K

The Rye

The Cadillac

The Friars Club

```
        ¹H
        U
        ²J
        ³D E A F
        S  C
        O  ⁴C      ⁵F      ⁶E
        ⁷K R A M E R      L
        E  T      I      A
        T  A      ⁸M A G I C
        L  O      R      N
                  ⁹C     ¹⁰S L E E P
   ¹¹W   ¹²G E O R G E
   E     A   M
   ¹³D A V I N C I
   D     G   C
   I     S
   N     T
   G     E
         R
```

The Calzone

```
              ¹T I ²P
                   A
              ³C   I
              I    S
              G    A
        ⁴N  ⁵G    N
        E   ⁶E L A I N E
   ⁷D   W   O    R    O
   ⁸K R A M E R  S    S
   Y   A   G
   ⁹P E N N ¹⁰I E ¹¹S
   R       T   ¹²P I Z Z A
           A   E
           ¹³I N F L U E N C E R
               I   D
           ¹⁴S T A D I U M
               N
               G
```

The Bottle Deposit

The Invitations

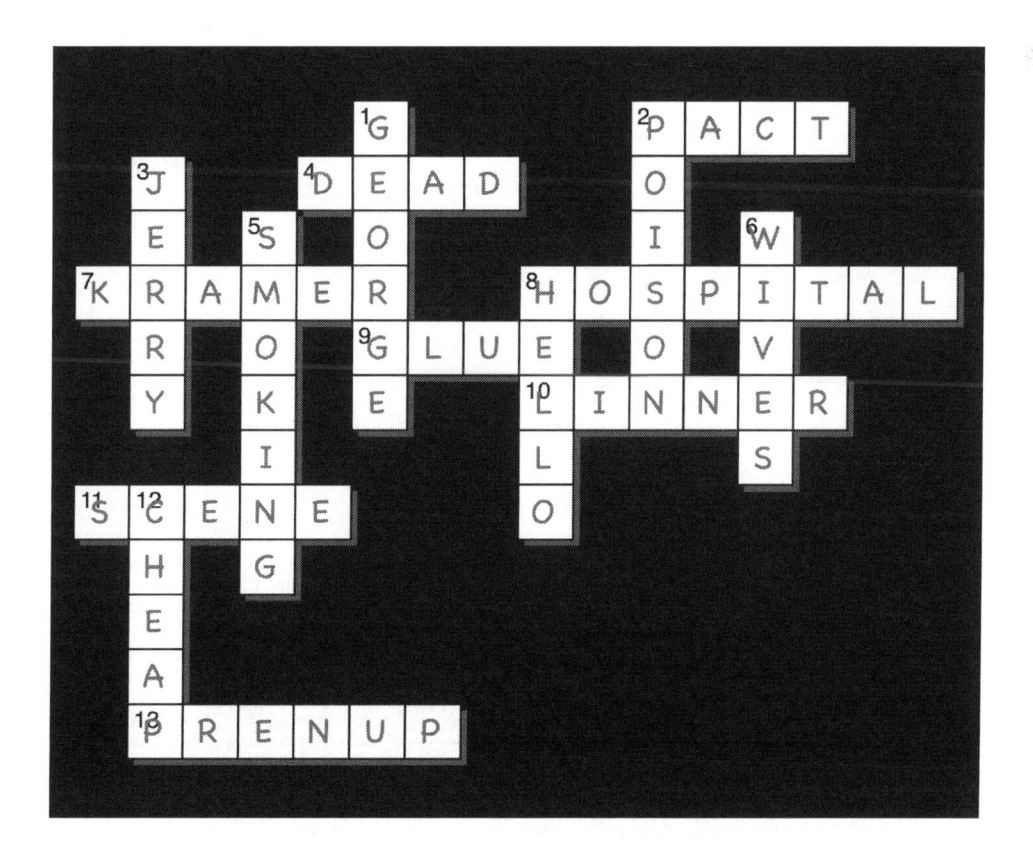

The Bizarro Jerry

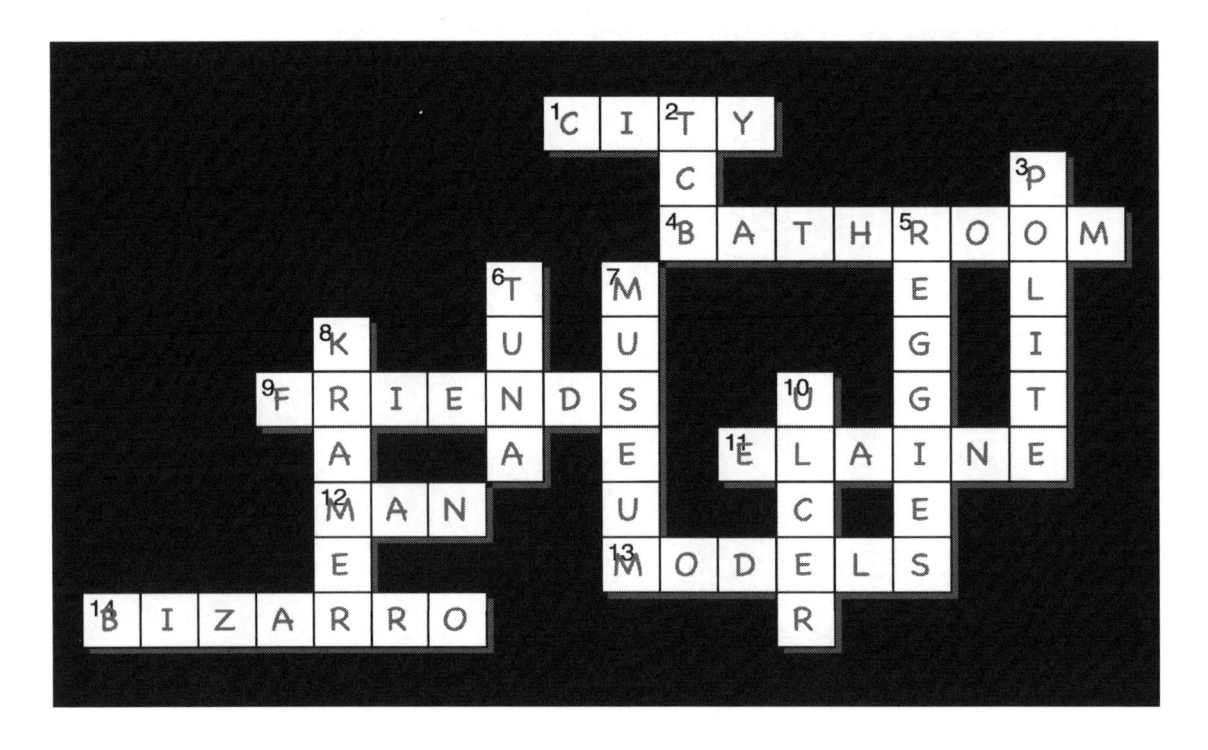

							¹C	I	²T	Y					
									C				³P		
							⁴B	A	T	H	⁵R	O	O	M	
				⁶T		⁷M				E		L		
		⁸K		U		U				G		I		
	⁹F	R	I	E	N	D	S		¹⁰U	G		T		
	A			A		S		¹¹E	L	A	I	N	E	
	¹²M	A	N			E			C					
	E				¹³M	O	D	E	L	S				
¹⁴B	I	Z	A	R	R	O			R					

The Abstinence

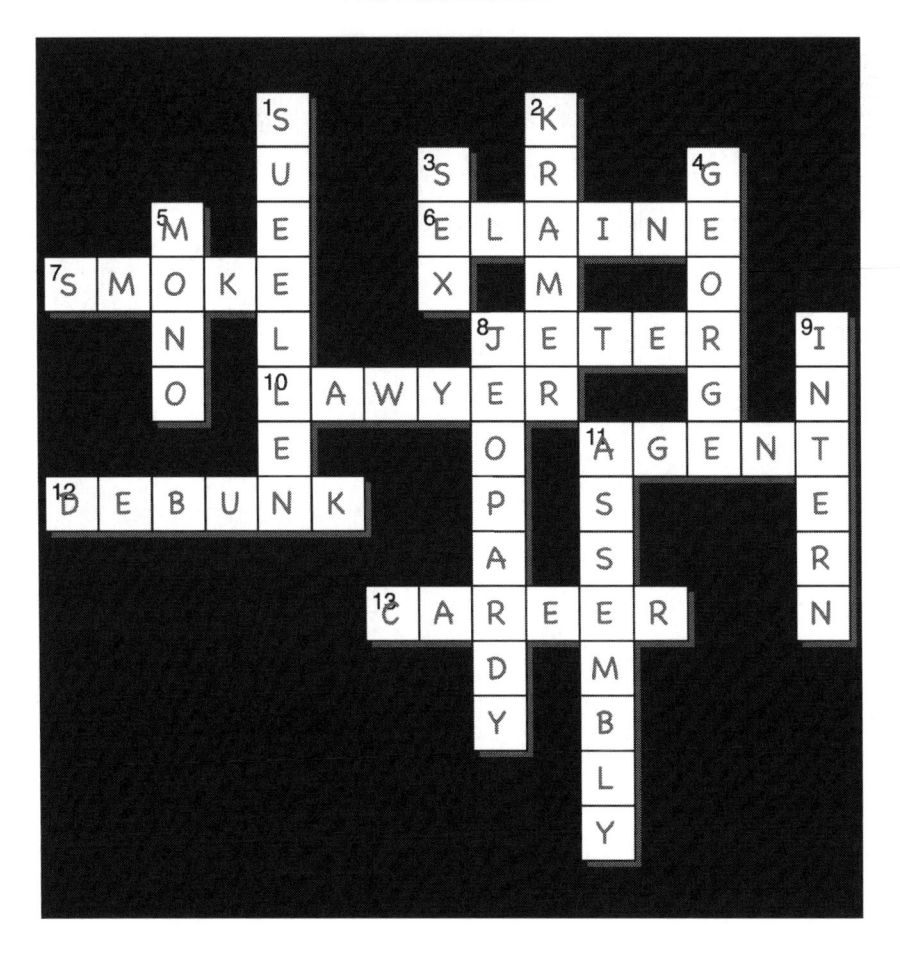

			¹S			²K			
			U		³S	R		⁴G	
		⁵M	E		⁶E	L	A	I	N	E
⁷S	M	O	K	E		X	M		O	
	N		L			⁸J	E	T	E	R	⁹I
	O	¹⁰L	A	W	Y	E	R		G		N
	E					O		¹¹A	G	E	N	T
¹²D	E	B	U	N	K		P		S			E
							A		S			R
				¹³C	A	R	E	E	R			N
							D		M			
							Y		B			
									L			
									Y			

The Yada Yada

			¹S		²D							
		³B	I	G	O	T						
	⁴E		N		U			⁵K				
	L				B			R				
	A				L			⁶A	D	O	P	T
	I				E			M				
⁷B	I	S	Q	U	E			⁸J	E	R	R	Y
N					D			E				
E			⁹F	A	T	H	E	R				
					T			W				
			¹⁰D	E	N	T	I	S	T			
			W					H				
¹¹D	E	B	R	A								
			A									
			R									
			F									

The Summer Of George

		¹E					²S	
		L					A	
		A			³W		⁴F	I R E D
		I					R	
	⁵I	N	V	I	T	E	I	D
		E					S	I
				⁶C		L	C	S
			⁷R	E	H	A	B	
			A			E	⁸A	⁹X
			Z		¹⁰G	E	O R G E
¹¹C	A	¹²T	T	Y			M	R
		O					¹³S H O W
		N						X
		Y						

The Serenity Now

The Merv Griffin Show

The Strike

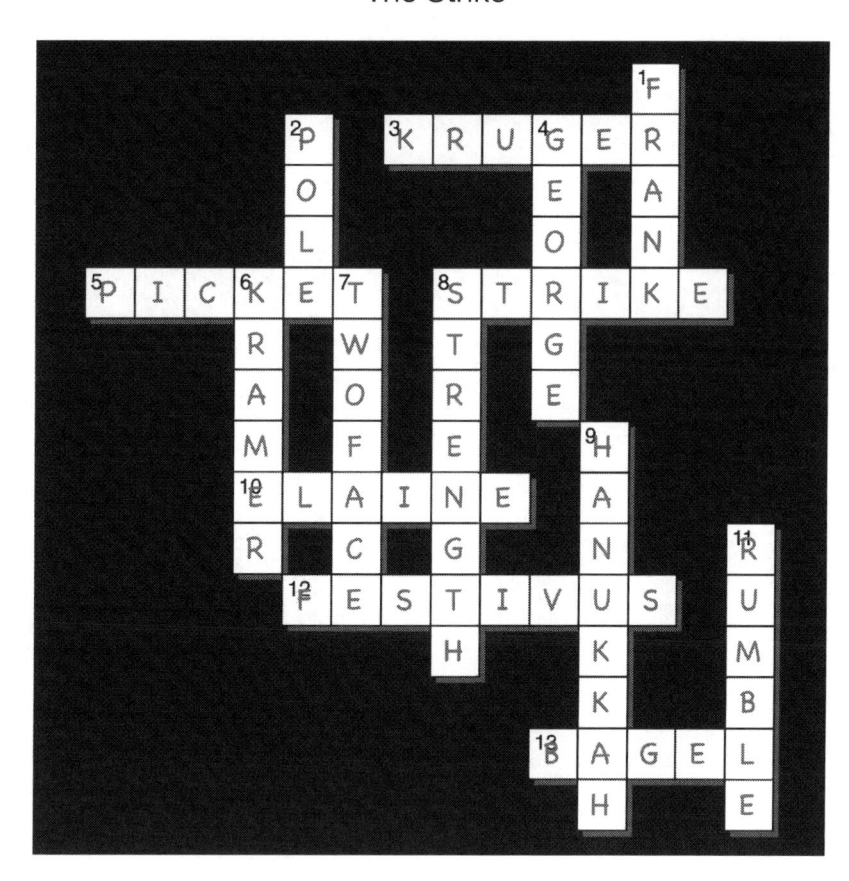

The Finale

Other Books by Miranda Powell

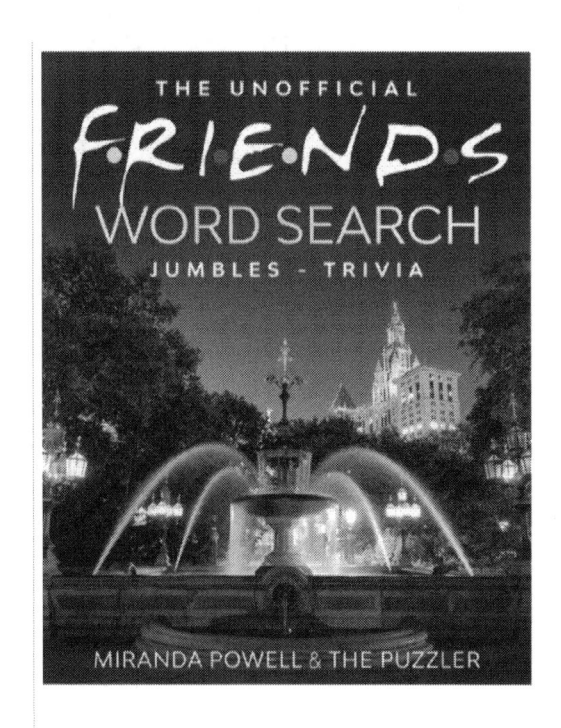

THE UNOFFICIAL JEOPARDY!
QUIZ SEARCH, JUMBLES, WORD SEARCH, TRIVIA

MIRANDA POWELL

THE UNOFFICIAL GREAT BRITISH BAKING SHOW
WORD SEARCH, JUMBLES, TRIVIA

MIRANDA POWELL

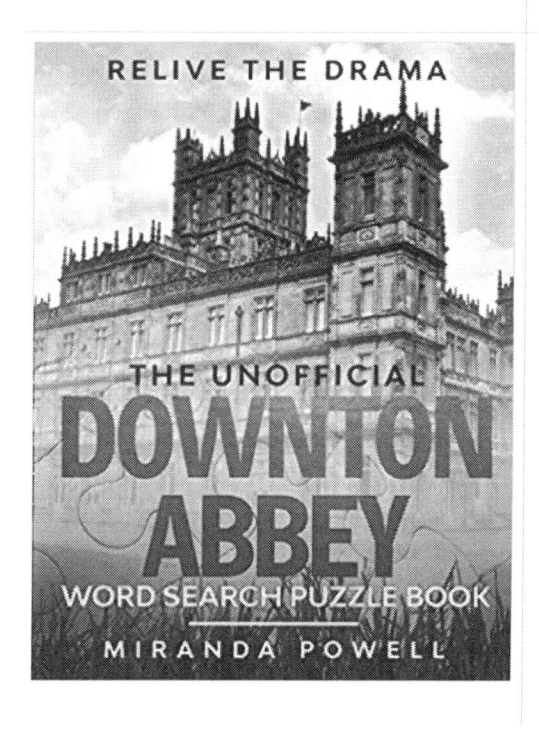

RELIVE THE DRAMA
THE UNOFFICIAL DOWNTON ABBEY
WORD SEARCH PUZZLE BOOK

MIRANDA POWELL

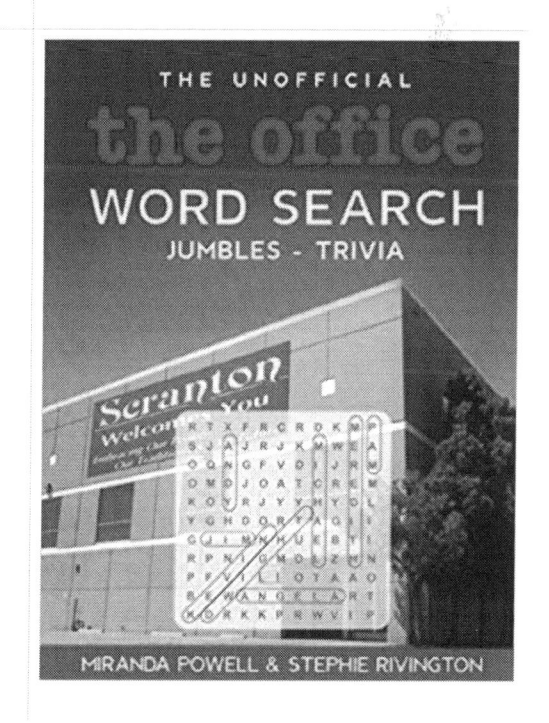

THE UNOFFICIAL the office
WORD SEARCH
JUMBLES - TRIVIA

MIRANDA POWELL & STEPHIE RIVINGTON

Thank again for purchasing this book. I hope it brought you hours of enjoyment.

As a small publishing company, reviews are the lifeblood of our continued success. If you could take a few minutes to leave us a review on Amazon it would be greatly appre iated.

www.oldtownpublishing.com/reviews

Thank you,

Miranda

Made in the USA
Monee, IL
27 November 2021